THE WAY OF THE CROSS

A Story of
Padre Pio

THE WAY OF THE CROSS

A Story of
Padre Pio

By
Claire Jordan Mohan

Illustrated by Jane Robbins

HILLSIDE EDUCATION

Copyright © Estate of Claire Jordan Mohan

Reprinted by Permission 2021 Hillside Education

All rights reserved. No part of this publication may be reproduced in whole or in part, stored in a retrieval system or transmitted in any form or by any means, electronic, mechanical, photocopying, recording, or otherwise, without prior written permission of the publisher.

Interior book design by Mary Jo Loboda

ISBN: 978-1-955402-01-9

Hillside Education
475 Bidwell Hill Road
Lake Ariel, PA 18436
www.hillsideeducation.com

Contents

1. A Special Child 1
2. Little Francisco 9
3. Boyhood Days 17
4. Growing Up in Pietrelcina- A New Birth 25
5. A New Life 37
6. Padre Pio 47
7. The Stigmata 55
8. A Poor Friar Who Prays 63
9. An Impossible Dream 71
10. In Jesus You Will Find Me 77
    Postscript 81
    Chronology 83
    A Miracle 85
    Padre Pio's Prayer 87

"Always live under the eyes of the Good Shepherd and you will walk unharmed through evil pastures."

Padre Pio

Chapter 1

A Special Child

Boys and girls, this is a mystery story. There are no spies, or murders. There are no secret codes, no hidden treasures. This is one of God's mysteries. Wherever it is told, everyone is awed, amazed—and, yes, puzzled. I think you will be, too.

How could he ever forget the date—September 20, 1918? Looking back, years later, he would still remember every detail. He was alone in the dark choir loft that afternoon. It was a day that changed his life forever. Padre Pio was a good and holy young man who lived a quiet prayerful life in the Franciscan monastery, but the events of that day would make him known throughout the world. Yes, God was working through him in a strange way—one, which changed not only his life, but that of all who would come to know him. Why did it happen to him? He loved God, but he had always been an ordinary boy.

First, let us go back a few years in time and get to know the young lad that he once was. Our story takes us to south central Italy. There, you would find Pietrelcina, a small town built on the side of a hill with cobblestone streets and little stone houses built close to the ground to protect them from earthquakes. A cluster of these poor homes surrounds a small ancient castle.

If you were to go there today, you would find it has changed little in the years since this little boy was living and playing there.

At 9 o'clock on the morning of May 25, 1887, as the church bells of St. Mary of the Angels Church were chiming, in one of those stone homes a little boy was born to Grazio and Maria Forgione. His brother, Michele, who was almost three years old at the time, was in the silent living room, waiting, listening to the unfamiliar sounds coming from the bedroom. He sat on his father's lap on the old rocking chair, which seemed to be moving back and forth faster than usual.

"Papa, where is my mama? Is mama okay?" the

little boy asked as he gazed up at his dad.

Before his dad could answer, they heard a strange cry. A few minutes later, the bedroom door opened and the midwife came into the room holding a tiny figure wrapped in a soft blanket. Grazio jumped from the chair, almost dumping his little son onto the floor.

"It's a boy!" she exclaimed as she placed a little infant in his papa's arms.

"How is Maria doing?" he asked her.

"Ah, she is fine, just a little sleepy," she replied.

With that he leaned down to show his son a squealing red-faced baby "Michele, look at your little brother. Isn't he handsome?"

"Come on, you two, Maria is waiting," the midwife called as she strode back into the bedroom.

Though the room was dark, sunlight poured through a single window onto the bed where his mother lay, looking very tired. On the bureau were a basin of water, a pitcher, and other objects strange to the little boy.

Like a little monkey, Michele climbed onto the bed of wrinkled sheets, "Mama, I love you," he whispered as he cuddled up next to her. Grazio, still holding his tiny son, sat on the side of the bed close to his wife. As he leaned down and kissed her hair. Maria pulled him and her little sons close to her and smiled.

The midwife, who was plumping the pillow and straightening the sheets, smiled at the little family. Now that everyone was settled, she was bursting with news for the glowing parents. She took the baby in her arms, held it up like a treasure, and turned to them.

"Maria, Grazio," she proclaimed proudly, "your son was born wrapped in a white veil! Do you know what this means?" Like bewildered birds, they shook their heads.

"It is a sign—a sign that he will either be great or very fortunate in life! He is special! I have never seen this before in all my days!

Grazio and Maria looked at each other. They knew this child was special. All parents feel that way about their children. They wondered at this news, but they did not understand. How could they? How could they know the future?

Grazio kissed his wife again and held her hand. Tears rolled down his cheek.

"Maria, let's say our thanks. God has blessed us."

Like moths to a flame, they turned their faces to the beloved crucifix hanging on the wall over the bed and knelt down. Little Michele clasped his small hands together and snuggled close to his parents. Maria reached under the pillow and pulled out her amber rosary. Together, they prayed.

Maria and Grazio were young parents in their early twenties. They worked hard together raising many crops and animals on their five-acres of barren soil to support their growing family. After their prayers, they did not think much about this news. They had a new son! They cradled the baby in their arms and admired him. The infant let out a yell and waved his tiny hands in the air.

"Oh, he is a healthy one," said the smiling midwife as she patted the little head.

"Grazio, isn't he beautiful!" Maria's blue eyes sparkled as she pushed dark hair from the little forehead and pulled her precious bundle close to her.

The next day around noon, the proud father and godparents, dressed in their Sunday finery, walked down the cobbled stone street to the nearby church of St. Mary. Grazio carried his new son bundled like a butterfly in a cocoon in the soft white shawl his mother had just finished crocheting. As was the custom in those days, his wife remained at home resting on the couch. They entered the dark church and walked up the aisle to the Baptismal Font where the priest greeted them. He had placed a golden crucifix nearby. Candles, like guardian angels, lit the area. Father anointed the little child with oil and poured the cool water on the sleeping baby's head.

He said the ritual prayers then asked, "By what name shall we call this child?"

"His name is Francisco," the godmother replied.

Chapter 2
LITTLE FRANCISCO

Francisco is his name. St. Francis of Assisi was Maria and Grazio's favorite saint and they wished their son to be like him. Though they felt they were blessed and the midwife had predicted that he would be great, this young child did not start out that way. He was not a happy baby! His dad toiled from sunrise till sunset on his farm. All day he cared for sheep, goats, hens, ducks, rabbits, and some hogs. On the land he raised grapes, wheat, corn, olives, figs, and plums. Though Maria, and eventually the children, helped out, it was hard work and this farmer was weary when he came home at the end of his day. Baby Francis often tried his father's patience by crying and screaming all night long. One particularly bad evening, Maria asked her husband, "Graz, would you please get up with the baby tonight? I am so tired."

"Of course, Mia, get your rest. I'll take care of him," her dutiful husband replied.

Maria rolled to her side and Grazio settled down on the bed next to the cradle where the restless baby lay. Within minutes, the baby started screaming. Grazio rocked the cradle gently. Still he cried. His dad picked him up and held him in his arms, singing a soft lullaby. The baby screamed. He took the child in his arms and walked back and forth and back and forth as the floor creaked beneath his feet. The baby screamed louder. Finally, Grazio could take it no longer! He tossed the infant onto the bed back to the exhausted mother.

He shouted, "Maria, it is the devil that has been born in my home!"

Before she could grasp him, the baby slipped from the bed and rolled onto the hard floor with a piercing cry.

"Grazio, what have you done?" Maria screamed.

She picked little Francisco up and held him close to her murmuring softly. She nursed him until he finally closed his eyes and fell asleep.

Sadly, fathers do not always know how to calm little babies in the middle of the night. Grazio tried his best, but it was not enough for Francisco—he wanted his mother. This kind man loved his children and would do anything for them and for his wife. He never lost his temper. Unlike many parents at that time who could be harsh, Grazio used persuasion and scolding, not spanking when his children misbehaved.

The Forgione's survived those early days with Francis and soon he had three little sisters, Felicita, Pelligrena, and Grazella. The children were taught to be prayerful and to love God. Each morning, the family would get up at dawn and say their morning prayers before they took the half-hour walk to the farm. Every evening at sunset, they would stop in church on their way home to thank God for His blessing and pray the rosary. It seemed Grazio always had his rosary in his hands!

In their small home a picture of the Blessed Mother was on the living room wall. Imitating their parents, the children often knelt before it as they recited their Hail Marys and fingered the beads. Life was centered on Jesus, His mother, and the saints. They followed the Commandments and knew they must not speak irreverently or use crude language and never worked on Sunday.

Franci began to show his love and respect for the Lord when he was still a little boy. When he was about five years old, the family was at a gathering at the home of a friend. All the children had to perch politely on the sofa by the window like little caged birds though they longed to be free outside. The women gathered together nearby sewing and discussing their children; the fathers lingered in the kitchen having a drink and smoking their pipes. When the little boy heard someone call out God's name in vain, he jumped from his seat and hid behind the door. His mother glanced over and saw him.

"Franci, what's wrong?" she queried as she ran to him.

"Mama, Mama," he cried as tears ran down his cheeks, "I just heard Luigi's papa insult God!"

Gathering him in her arms, Maria took him outside and comforted him, "Don't cry. Babe," she said. "It will be okay. We will say a little prayer together that God will forgive him."

Franci did like to pray. One evening he was at his grandmother's when the Angelus bells sounded. Grandma gathered up her black shawl and her prayer book and started out the door. Francis ran after her.

"Grandma, I want to go to church with you," the little boy stated.

His aunt interrupted, "Wait a minute, Franci, you haven't had your supper yet."

"I don't care," he responded with a stamp of his foot. "I want to go to church with my grandmother."

Ah, but Franci was not an angel. As he grew older, he was the usual big brother, the kind who needs a good scolding once in a while. He had three sisters that he often teased.

There was no bathroom with toilet, shower, or tub in the Forgione's little home. Once a week at bedtime the children would wash in a portable tub placed in the kitchen. There was also no water piped or pumped in so three times a day Maria would have to climb up and down twenty steps to carry some home. The spring water was icy so Maria would warm a bucketful in the fireplace and pour it in the tub so the children could bathe. Each child would get a turn in the warm soapy suds. After they washed themselves she would wrap them in a towel, and put them to bed.

When his mother would leave the room. Franci would sneak up behind one of his sisters, as she washed herself.

"Mama, Mama, he's doing it again!" She would scream as her brother laughed. Soap would burn her eyes and water splashed all over the wooden floor.

"Mama, Franci is dunking my head. Mama, make him stop!" Maria would come running.

"Franci, come with me. You know better than that," she would scold him as she grabbed him by the ear and sent him to bed. "Leave your sister alone!" And he wouldn't do it again—until the next time!

Chapter 3
BOYHOOD DAYS

Although usually a kind and loving child, like you and all boys and girls, Francis wasn't perfect. He didn't like it when his friends mistreated him. One hot summer afternoon while the sun was blazing in the afternoon sky, he was napping like a contented puppy outside under a shady tree. His friend, Mercurio, spied him taking a siesta and saw some dried corn stalks lying in the field nearby.

"Ah," he thought, "I will have some fun."

With that, he took the stalks and completely covered the sleeping boy head to toe. Then he hid behind the tree waiting to enjoy his trick.

A few minutes later, Franci woke up and was very frightened by the darkness. He didn't know where he was. He could hardly breathe.

"Mama, Mama," he screamed as he pushed aside the scratchy covering.

Mercurio laughed as he ran away and called out loudly, "Baby. Baby!"

A day later, Franci was outside behind the house playing catch with his dog, Principe. As he was throwing the ball, he noticed his friend taking a siesta on top of a small farm wagon. It was his chance to get even. He carefully pulled the wagon with the dozing youngster up a nearby hill and shoved it. Mercurio suddenly awakened as he flew down the hill. This time he did the screaming.

"Help! Help!" he cried as the wagon sped along until it crashed into a tree and stopped. Franci watched from the top of the hill. Mercurio was not hurt, but he dashed home to tell his mother—and he never tormented Franci again.

Francis tried to be a good child always listening to his parents when they told him what was right. He and his friend, Luigi, loved to wrestle. They were often found in the meadow on the soft grass enjoying this sport that boys everywhere seem to relish. One day, after a hard fight, Franci pinned Luigi down. Luigi swore in exasperation. As soon as he heard these words, Franci released him, jumped up, and flew home as fast as his legs would carry him.

Luigi, puzzled, called after him. "Hey, Fran, I'm okay. Where are you going.

There was no answer. Franci did not turn back. Later that day, as the village boys were gathered on the court after supper, the two faced each other again. This time Franci answered Luigi's question.

He told him solemnly, "It's simple, Luigi. My mother taught me that I shouldn't use bad language and I must leave if anyone else does, so I did."

Another time on a quiet Sunday afternoon when he was a little older, he was ambling thoughtfully down the cobblestone lane to visit his cousins. He passed the home of the old shoemaker who always chatted with him. He looked toward the house hoping to see him by the window. No one waved, but he noticed the man's daughter sitting in the doorway with a needle in her hand sewing a band on her dress. Now, you have to remember that life was different at that time. Sunday was a peaceful day. Everyone worked very hard during the week. This seventh day they went to church, visited with their family and friends, or just rested. Stores were closed and no one would do any cleaning, sewing, or servile work. When Franci noticed she was stitching, he worried about her committing a sin. He ran to the girl and cautioned her.

"Andrianella, today we don't work. It's Sunday."

The girl looked up and saw her little neighbor. She shook her finger at him as she continued to sew.

"Little boy, you are too small to talk to me like that," she retorted.

Francis hurried home and got a pair of scissors. He ran up to Andrianella, snatched the band she had been sewing and cut it into pieces.

The girl cried out, "Francis, you little imp, what are you doing! Give me my dress!"

She grabbed him and her dress. Francis pulled away from the angry girl, satisfied that he had saved her soul, and continued down the street.

On another walk, Francis himself learned a lesson. One day, a neighbor called to him as he was going to the store for his mother.

"Here, Franci, will you pick up a cigar for me?" He pulled out some coins.

"Sure," Franci answered.

He purchased the groceries for his mother and the cigar. In fact, he bought two cigars, one for himself. On the way home, he lit up. After one puff, he felt so sick he couldn't go another step without throwing up. He sat down on a large rock under an olive tree by the side of the road until his stomach stopped feeling queasy. When the sickness finally passed, he tried standing up. Feeling steady on his feet, he started up the lane once more. He tossed the cigar away, and promised himself, "I'll never ever do that again!"

Though he seemed to be a healthy boy, when he was ten years old Franci became ill with typhus, a disease which causes coughing, headache, chest pain and sudden high fever and chills. He was so sick he could hardly lift up his head. His mother tried everything she could think of to make him better. She sent for the village doctor who came right out and examined the boy. Though he tried many medications, there were no antibiotics in those days. Nothing helped poor Franci.

"I'm sorry, Mama Peppe, I can't do anything more to cure this lad. We must leave it in the hands of God. His parents prayed all the time, but he just got worse.

"Oh, Papa, what is going to happen to our little

boy," worried Maria. "Is God going to take him from us?"

Maria who loved God and always accepted His will, couldn't bear the thought of losing her child. She spent hours by his bedside, placing wet cloths on his forehead and giving him cool drinks, but she still had other work to do. Every day she had to prepare meals for the harvesters at the farm. One day she made a huge platter of fried peppers for the helpers. The men came to the table and ate greedily, but enough was left over for the Forgione family's next meal.

"Grazio and the children will really enjoy this for supper. I'll save it in the cupboard," she thought.

The fragrance of this delicious food flew like an arrow through the house right to Francis nose. Even though he hadn't eaten for days, he loved fried peppers! He was drawn to the smell. As soon as his mother left the house, he slipped out of bed, crawled over to the cupboard, and downed all the peppers.

"Oh, these are so good," he murmured to himself. When his mother came home, she found the empty platter on the table.

"Michele, come here this minute," she scolded. "Why did you let the dog in? He cleaned the plate and all our supper is gone! Wait till your papa hears about this!"

Michele was startled. "But, Mama..." he began.

Before he could finish his sentence, Francis called to his mother from his bed.

"Mama," he apologized, "Don't blame Michele or Principe. It was me."

"I ate the peppers!"

Just then his hungry father burst in the door. Maria hugged him. "Oh, Grazio! God has blessed us. Franci is eating again!" she cried out.

No one knows how or why, but for some reason known only to God, Francis got better instantly and was cured of the typhus!

Chapter 4

Growing Up in Pietrelcina- A New Birth

Though, as we have seen, Francisco was an ordinary boy with his good and bad moments, God had special plans for him as He has for all of us if we listen to Him. From the time he was very little, Francis would have visions of Jesus and Mary. He saw his guardian angel so often that he called the angel "the playmate of my life." Other times his visions were frightening, but all these appearances happened so often, he just thought all children had them and didn't tell anyone about them, not even his brother or sisters.

His religious life was something like yours. When Francis was ten years old, he made his First Holy Communion and was confirmed when he was twelve. As an altar boy he was happy to serve the priest any time he was needed. His parents were proud of him and his mother often heard her friends say, "Mamma Peppe, I wish my son was like your Franci."

Farm boys did not get much schooling. Too soon they were needed for work in the field. Francis studied in a little one-room schoolhouse where the children just learned to read and write and do a little math. There was no grammar, science, or social studies, and no hours of homework like children have today. But Franci was eager to learn and practiced on his own. Each day as the sheep wandered about devouring the grass, Franci would find himself a comfortable spot high enough to keep his eye on his charges. Then he would open a book and read out loud to the animals who wandered near him.

Parents taught their children to love God and the saints and showed them how to live by His

Commandments. Each Sunday the village children went to the priest's house next to the ivy-covered church after Mass. As they sat in his book-lined study, he told them Bible stories, taught them catechism, and prepared them for the sacraments.

Mama and Papa Forgione were very faithful Catholics. They prayed every day and often journeyed with their little ones to nearby shrines. One year Francis' father took him to the shrine of St. Pellegrina. The church was filled with pilgrims hoping for a cure. Francis pushed his way through the crowd that filled the aisles and found a front pew close to the altar where he knelt to pray. He was distracted by loud weeping and noticed a woman carrying a crippled little boy.

The woman stared at St. Pellegrina's statue and kept calling out, "Heal my son! Heal my son!"

Francis couldn't take his eyes off her. He silently joined his prayers with hers.

"Dear God, please make this child better," he pleaded, but nothing happened.

"Francis, we have to go now," his father told him as he pulled on his son's sleeve.

"Wait just a minute. Papa, please," he begged.

As Francis continued to pray, he was horrified to see the mother pick up her frightened child and throw him onto the saint's altar.

"If you don't want to cure him, take him! I don't want him!" she screamed.

As soon as the little boy landed on the altar, a strange thing happened. He stood up on strong legs and called to his mother, "Mama, Mama!" It was a miracle! The mother wept as she clutched her child and held him close to her. Francis could only stare at the scene before him. Word quickly spread throughout the shrine and a large group gathered around them. Grazio marched up to his son and pulled at his sleeve again.

"Franci," he pronounced. "I told you we have to leave. Now let's go. I am tired of waiting for you."

This time the boy did jump up quickly, but he never forgot the miracle that had happened before his eyes and couldn't wait to tell his mama and brother.

Although he loved the land as much as his friends, Francis knew he wanted to be a priest, not a farmer, when he grew up. When he was about ten years old, while in church listening to a sermon on St. Michael the Archangel, he knew God was calling him. He came running down the street, almost tripping on the cobblestones in his hurry to tell his parents. He burst in the door and startled his parents who were sitting at the table drinking glasses of goat's milk.

"Mama, Papa. I'm going to be a priest!" he exclaimed.

"Now, Franci, calm down. What are you talking about? You're just a little boy," said his father. "When you get older, we'll talk about this.

Still, Franci did not give up or forget. That same year, Friar Camilio, a Franciscan monk came to Pietrelcina seeking alms for the poor. His sermon at Mass struck Franci's heart. He was mesmerized. Then he knew for sure what he was meant to do. That night as the family was finishing supper, Franci pushed his plate away.

"Mama, Papa," he stated, "listen to me. When I grow up, I want to serve God like Friar Camilio with the long handsome beard.

His father and mother put down their forks. Michele and the girls did the same. For a moment all were silent. Then Grazio looked at Maria with a question in his eyes. The floor squeaked as he pushed back his sturdy chair, stood, and moved toward his son.

"Franci, don't worry," he said as he patted the boy on the head. "If you do your schoolwork well, we will see to it that you become a monk.

From then on the Forgione family began to talk more and more about his future.

In school Francisco only learned the basics of reading and writing and arithmetic. His father knew if he was to be a priest, he needed a real education, but private tutors were expensive. Farmers didn't make much money.

"I have been thinking about our son," Grazio told

his wife, "There is only one way we can do it, Mama. I'll have to go to America and work. I hate to leave you and the children to work the farm for months without me, but how else can we pay for a tutor?"

"Graz, don't worry, we'll manage," she replied as she embraced him.

They hired a local educator to work with their son, but somehow Francis was not making progress. His mama, who knew Franci was a smart boy, did not understand.

The tutor told her, "Mrs. Forgione. I think this is all too hard for your son. Think about it. He may not be suited for the priesthood. Your boy does not seem interested and is distracted while I am teaching."

When Maria questioned Franci, he told her, "Mama, I don't like him. How can he teach me? He was a priest, but now he doesn't even go to church!"

Grazio was in America when Maria sent him a letter telling him what was going on. He sent a telegram to his wife, "Change teachers immediately." Maria did as he said and as soon as Francis started work with the new tutor things turned around. He studied hard and after a couple of years, he applied to enter the Capuchin Franciscan Monastery.

The letter of admission came when he was not yet 16. Francis was accepted to study for the priesthood! Though he had waited for this day, Francis was still a young man and he had mixed emotions. He loved family life. He loved living, laughing, and praying with his brothers and sisters. He loved his mama and papa.

"I'm only fifteen," he thought, "maybe I should wait until I'm older."

But the date was set and everything was ready. During his last night at home he felt very sad. He lay on his bed crying. Christ came to comfort him.

He was told he was being "assigned a great mission known only to God and himself." He saw by his side a majestic man of rare beauty, splendid as the sun. This man took him by the hand and he heard him say, "Come with me, because you will have to fight as a valiant warrior." Our Lord placed His hand upon Francis head, giving him the special strength for the days ahead. He gained courage and fell asleep with peace in his heart.

On January 6, 1903, Francisco Forgione left Pietrelcina with two other boys from his area. His little sisters stood at the door and cried. His brother placed his bag on the wagon and their horse pulled them to the train station.

As they stood on the platform, his Mama kissed him. Tears streamed down her cheeks. The whistle sounded and she gave him a long last hug.

"Franci, I love you. Be careful now, be good. Remember you now belong to God."

"Don't worry, Mama. I'll be okay," he told her as he wiped her tears with his new white handkerchief.

He grabbed his bag, joined his friends, and stepped aboard, waving as the train chugged away. An hour later the train pulled into Morcone Station. The boys were met by an old man and taken in a cart to the friary of Saints Philip and James. Friar Camillo, Franci's hero, met them at the door.

"Welcome, boys," he stated, "Come in, put your things over there, and I will show you around."

After a tour of the grounds and the chapel, Franci was taken to room 28. He looked inside. The first thing he saw in his cell (as the room was called) was a crucifix on the wall. It made him feel at home. Exhausted from all the new experiences, he dropped onto a trestle with a straw mattress and closed his eyes. Later, as he got up when a bell signaled prayer, he noticed a chair by the window, and a very small table holding the Bible, and a few other books. With his two friends and the monks, Francis went to the chapel. Fifteen days later on January 22, he received the religious habit and Francis Forgione began a new life with a new name symbolizing his new birth—Fra Pio da Pietrelcina.

Chapter 5
A New Life

Fra Pio was still a boy who had a lot to learn. Life in the friary was far different than the life he was used to at home and on the farm with his brothers and sisters. Overcome with love of God and fascinated by the Franciscan monks, he had never dreamt things in the monastery would be so different—but different they were!

Luckily Francis didn't require a lot of food, as on most days the monks didn't concern themselves with what they ate. They fasted every Friday and throughout Lent and Advent. There was no heat and they even had to sleep wearing their heavy dark robes. Prayers were scheduled throughout the day. At midnight, they all were awakened by the clang of a bell to pray in the chapel with the friars. Each day there were instructions about their new life as future monks. And, hardest of all, they were not allowed to talk except for a short time when they had recreation! Francis was a lively boy of fifteen used to physical work on the farm and lots of fun with his brother and sisters. Yet, the novice master told his parents Fra Pio was a "novice without reproach."

He tried to be the best friar that he could be. He tried so hard that one time his actions hurt the one he loved the most. A few weeks after he entered, Maria came to visit her son. After a long ride on the train, she arrived tired, but excited, at the monastery. She rang the bell and was welcomed by one of the brown-robed friars.

"Come; follow me," she was told as she walked with him to a bench in the garden. Nearby, a statue of St. Francis of Assisi smiled down on her. The birds were chirping loudly and she could hardly wait to see Francis. She knew he would be pleased with his favorite treats and the gifts from the children, which she carried in her bag. Imagine her sadness when her son came into sight. He didn't run to her. He didn't hug or kiss her. He kept his eyes cast down and his arms were folded with his hands buried in the sleeves of his brown robe. Maria reached her arms out to him.

"Franci," she pleaded, "It's me, your mama. Don't you recognize me? What's wrong?"

An eagle swooped down from the blue sky searching for his prey.

Francis didn't say a word. After a short time when she did all the talking, Maria reached for her bag and stared at this strange young man who was her son."

"Franci," she implored. "I don't understand what's happened to you. Can't you talk?"

A cool breeze ruffled the leaves of the nearby trees and a drop of rain fell on her cheek. Maria shivered. Dabbing her eyes with a handkerchief, she added, "Franci, I have to go."

She kissed his face and turned to the entrance gate shaken by her experience. She couldn't bear talking to anyone. Her son watched her as she hurried down the path, but still he said nothing. She cried all the way home.

"I have got to talk to Grazio," she told herself as she looked out the train's window at the valley beyond. "Wait until he hears about this!"

Her husband had just returned from America

a short time before the visit. When Maria finally reached her station, her husband was there to meet her. He was looking forward to hearing about his son. As she stepped down to the platform, he immediately noticed that her eyes were red.

"Maria, what's wrong?" he asked.

"Papa," she told him, "It's Franci! He wouldn't talk to me. He wouldn't even look at me! Oh, Grazio, if I had known he would act that way, I would never have gone. I would have just stayed home."

Grazio took her hand and helped her onto the wagon. "Mia, stay calm now. I'll get to the bottom of this. We'll talk about it when we get home."

Darkness had fallen. Already the children were sleeping. Maria made a hot drink and they sat at the kitchen table sipping their cups while she told her husband all that happened. Grazio ran his fingers through his hair.

"Something is radically wrong, Maria. I'll go to the friary tomorrow. Franci is going to wreck his health. Oh, dear Lord, I hope he is not losing his mind!"

When Grazio arrived at the friary the next day, he spoke to the novice master.

"Father, what is going on with my son?" he asked.

"He wouldn't even talk to his mother."

"Ah," he was told, "Pio is a good young man. I think he felt that is what he was supposed to do. I will talk to him. He is trying too hard to be a saint. Come, let's go see him and straighten this out."

As the novice master urged him, Pio responded to his fathers greeting. With tears in his eyes, he said he was sorry and sent his love home to his mother.

While we know that Pio was determined to be saintly, there were times he was still a boy at heart and couldn't help himself. Just as he had, in fun, dunked his sister's head in the soapy water of the bathtub, he played tricks on the other novices. One night when he was returning from midnight prayers and the bathroom, he noticed one of his friends coming down the dark hallway. He hid behind a nearby table that had on it two candlesticks and a human skull. As the other novice passed by, Pio groaned and flapped his towel at the boy.

"Oh, God help me," he cried in fear.

"Wait! It's only me," Pio told him, trying to quiet him before they got into trouble. The boy just ran faster toward his room. Just as Pio finally caught up with him, the other boy tripped and fell. Pio tumbled on top of him. At first the other boy was too scared to recognize him, but in minutes they both laughed and went to bed without being caught.

In between chapel visits, studies, and midnight romps, the boys prayed on their own. Pio loved to say the rosary as he had always done each night at home. It was his favorite prayer to his "other Mama." He and his friend Fra Anastasio decided to have a contest to see who could say the most rosaries in one day. He said he would try to say fifteen. One night he woke up when he heard sounds in the next room. He thought Fra Anastasio must still be up reciting the rosary. So Fra Pio fell to his knees to keep up the contest. As he prayed, he looked out at Anastasio's window. Suddenly, he was shocked to see a huge black dog with eyes glowing like embers leave the room and take a big leap to a nearby roof and disappear. He fell on his bed feeling faint. The next day Anastasio told him that he had moved to another room. His friend was puzzled, but Pio, who had often had frightening visions, was not!

One year after his entrance, almost seventeen years old, Pio made his first vows of poverty, chastity, and obedience. Now it was time for serious study to become a priest, but Pio became ill. Just as when he had had typhus as a little boy, nothing seemed to help him.

"Fra Pio," his superior told him, "we think it would be a good idea for you to study at home for a while until you get your health back. The warm climate may cure you."

He was sent back to Pietrelcina where his mother's home cooking and the love of his family made him feel well. Yet, as soon as he would return to the friary, he would get sick and had to go home again. He worried that he would be expelled from the Franciscans. His mother felt differently.

"Franci," she told him. "I think you should forget about the Franciscans and just stay here and help our village priest. I know I can make you better.

You belong here in Pietrelcina.

No one could figure out what was wrong with him. There seemed to be no hope for a cure. At times his temperature was up to 120°! Pio was surely dying. He wanted to be a priest before he died and asked for special permission. Finally, when he was twenty-three years old, his wish was granted. On a bright sunny day in August, amid the splendor of the Benevento

Cathedral, this young friar lay before the altar and was ordained a priest.

That night Maria wrote to her husband who was again in America:

> "Dearest Grazio," it began. "It was a wonderful day! The girls and I were so happy. If only you and Michele could have been here, it would have been perfect. Our Franci is really a priest! The ceremony was breathtaking. I couldn't stop the tears from rolling down my cheeks. I must have used up three handkerchiefs.
>
> When we came home, everyone in the village came to greet us as we got off the train. It was all so wonderful! Oh. I wish you were here! Tell Michele that his sweet wife even hired a band to meet us at the station!"

Four days later Francis sang his first High Mass in the church in Pietrelcina. Fra Pio was now Padre Pio.

Chapter 6
Padre Pio

Pio was now a priest—but still a sick one. He could not leave Pietrelcina, though he would often try. For about six years, he would return from time to time to the friary and try to live there. As soon as he settled in, he became so sick that he was sent back to his home and his family. While there he helped the local priest, Don Pannullo, by teaching catechism to the village children and giving spiritual counseling to the members of the church. He also studied, but most the time he spent in prayer in two special places. He had discovered a room high up on the mountain. He had to climb a steep stone stairway to reach this little tower. There, like an eagle in its nest, he was alone in silence. He also would go out to the countryside and sit beneath a shady beech tree whose limbs protected him from the hot sun. Like his model, St. Francis of Assisi, Pio would feel joy listening to the song of the birds as he spoke to God.

It was in September, only a month after his ordination while he was sitting under the tree that something strange happened. He had been praying to Jesus and Mary when he noticed a red spot the size of a nickel had appeared in the middle of each hand and at the same time there was pain on the bottoms of his feet. Pio wondered what was happening to him. He had to talk to someone who would understand. He jumped up from his resting-place, grabbed his prayer book, and ran to the village where he showed the marks to Pati, as he called the local priest he had known since he was an altar boy.

"Pio," he said. "This is very strange. Let's go right now to see the doctor. I just saw him go into his office down in the court."

They went first to that physician and then to another in the nearest town, but there was no explanation for the wounds. They returned to the rectory and sat on wooden chairs behind the house where they picked up the Bible. It opened to Psalm 66 and read. "You tested us, God, you refined us like silver, you laid heavy burdens on our backs.

"Pati," begged Pio, "You must pray with me. If this is from Jesus, then we must ask Him to take the wounds away. I don't mind suffering, even dying of suffering, for the Kingdom of God as long as it is a secret."

"Pio," Pati replied, "What if it is God's will?"

With that they hurried the few steps away to the church. They opened the heavy oak doors, strode up the aisle, and knelt together before the altar of Our Lady of the Angels. Stretching out their arms they prayed together in Jesus' words, "Father, if it be Thy will..." God heard their prayer, the visible wounds did go away, but for years Pio still had the red marks and agonizing pain in his palms and feet. Two years later, Padre Pio wrote in his journal, "From Thursday evening up to Saturday and on Tuesday also, a painful tragedy takes place. My heart, hands, and feet seem to be pierced through by a sword, so great is the pain I feel.

Though Pio suffered, God blessed him in many ways. He still had visions of Jesus and Mary and visits from his guardian angel just as when he was a child. One day Pio received a letter in Greek, a language he did not know. He read the letter and showed it to Pati.

"Pio, you never studied Greek. How can you read this?" he was asked.

"My guardian angel explained it all to me," was the reply.

Another time the same thing happened with a letter that had been sent in French. His guardian angel, "his playmate as a child," also came to comfort him when he had frightening visions from Satan.

During his years at home, Pio began giving spiritual direction by letter to men and women trying to come closer to God. He wrote hundreds of letters. The villagers began to call him a saint and even his superiors recognized his holiness and were turning to the young friar for advice.

Finally, after nearly seven years in Pietrelcina, on February 17, 1916 when he was twenty-nine, he returned to the friary. Many people came to him for confession and guidance, but he again became very ill. He had spells of vomiting and perspiring, and high fever. His fevers were so high that the mercury shot out of the thermometer and his temperature was recorded at an impossible 127.4° on an outdoor thermometer! Once again he was burning up and felt like he was going to die.

His superiors decided he needed a change of climate. They sent him to San Giovanni Rotondo, a mountain area, isolated and unknown to the world. The Capuchin friary was located two miles above a small town filled with poor homes and poor people living without any modern conveniences. There were no paved roads and the friary was reached by a mule-track used by shepherds.

His superiors hoped the clear fresh air would be good for him and he did feel better. After an eight-day rest he returned to the monastery and asked for permission to stay longer. This request was granted.

Unfortunately, his peaceful break was interrupted. The world about them was changing. Italy was swept into World War I and along with sixty other friars. Padre was drafted into the Italian army. Although sad to lay aside his habit, he remained cheerful and was happy to serve his country. But after about two weeks, he was found to be too ill to serve and was given a leave. Pio went back to his mountain-top haven.

Six months later, he was called back and served for three months, and again given a four-month leave. Finally, he was declared permanently unfit and discharged.

The officer told him, "I am sending you home to die."

But God had other plans. He was called back to San Giovanni Rotondo and became the spiritual director of boys in the small seminary. Confessions, meditations, and spiritual direction of these boys, who grew to love him, kept him busy.

The villagers got to know him too and he soon also had a group of local young women who came up the mountain twice a week as a group for talks on the spiritual life. They began attending his morning Mass and making him their confessor. They watched carefully to see how much time Pio gave to the others. Some, like jealous cats, complained when they saw that not all were receiving the same number of minutes. You know in your own life how you often tell your parents, "It's not fair. He got more than me!" Your parents, like the Heavenly Father, know what is best for each child. Eventually you come to learn that everyone is different and we must trust in God to give us what we truly need.

Padre Pio, like a loving parent, cared for his spiritual

children. He had the gift for reading minds and was aware of their complaints. Patiently he explained to them, "Some souls need only a quick reassuring pat on the back while others need a complete work-over. Some go to Paradise by train, others in a carriage, and still others on foot. I am here for you whichever way you go."

Chapter 7

THE STIGMATA

The word "stigmata" comes from the Greek word which means a sign or a mark.

What was God telling Padre Pio, and us, when he placed His sign upon Padre Pio? Why was he chosen and what are we to make of it? Why would God do this? As we continue our story, perhaps you will be able to answer these questions.

By September 1918, World War I was slowly coming to an end. German morale had crumbled and as the American army moved forward, the German government was advised to seek peace. At the same time a great flu epidemic, which killed millions, including Pio's sister Felicita, and her son, enveloped the world. But Padre Pio was not a part of that realm. Having been discharged from the army two years earlier, he had been living in the quiet of the friary at San Giovanni Rotondo where life does not change with the whims of human affairs.

On the 20th of the month, he was the only priest praying at the friary of our Lady of Grace. No one was sick there and it was even more silent than usual since one friar was out begging and the superior had gone to another friary on business. No other adult was home that morning. The students were in the library, busy with their studies, and Padre Pio was alone with God in the chapel.

It was early morning. The mist had left the mountain and the skies were pink with the morning sunrise. Pio had gone to the choir loft after he said Mass and he was kneeling before a big crucifix thanking God for all His goodness.

As he prayed, he stared at Jesus' face wracked with pain and blood streaming from the wounds on His head, hands, feet, and side. The loft was silent as a tomb: not even the morning song of a bird penetrated the stained glass windows. A feeling of peace came over him as he uttered his prayers. Then, like a flash of lightning, he saw before him a mysterious person similar to the one he had seen in another vision. The only difference was that this time his hands and feet and side were dripping real blood. The sight terrified him and he could hardly think. He felt he was dying. His heart was pounding so hard he thought it would burst through his chest. He was unable to move or pray and could barely breathe until he felt the Lord calm him. When the vision disappeared, he saw that his own hands, feet, and side were dripping blood!

This time, there was no way Padre Pio could keep the matter quiet. He dragged himself from the choir to his cell, leaving a trail of bright red blood all along the long hallway to his room. He was barely able to stand on his feet. He lay on his straw bed and tried to think.

"Dear Lord," he prayed, "What is happening to me?"

The sun was high in the sky. The seminarians were going to lunch. He heard the clacking of wagon wheels and the sound of voices outside his window and knew his superior had returned. He rose from his bed and as soon as he could collect his thoughts, he struggled to his superior's office. He showed him the bleeding wounds.

"My son," he was told, "I am overwhelmed. This

is all so strange. Let's go to the chapel and go over what happened. I'll contact the Provincial; we need his advice."

In that place and time, where telephones were a luxury and computers unheard of, the post office provided their only option. Letters, even airmail, would take days to reach their intended reader. The head of the Franciscans was very concerned about Padre Pio and wanted to make sure there was no deceit involved. He wondered if perhaps Pio was having a mental breakdown or another problem with his health. A meeting was called and within weeks the priests were consulting daily pondering this situation.

"This is not to leave the friary!" they all agreed. "It is a private matter for the Franciscan family."

As the days ran into months with still no change, it was decided that important medical men must examine Pio, who was embarrassed by all the attention and begged the Lord to take it away. This time God did not answer him. Pio was in agony every day; his heart bled constantly and he felt like he would bleed to death, but he did not complain. He said Mass daily and continued his life as a friar.

Finally, the important medical men were called. The head physician at the city of Barletta's hospital saw Padre Pio's five wounds in May 1919.

Another doctor sent by the cardinal studied Pio in June. In October a surgeon from Rome made his first examination of the stigmata. Other doctors who saw Pio's stigmata were Pope Benedict XV's personal physician and another who was also mayor of San Giovanni Rotondo. Though they tried to find an answer, they all came to the conclusion that the wounds had nothing to do with tuberculosis or any other mental or medical condition.

His wounds were deep. They seemed to be pierced all the way through and they should have either healed up or become infected with gangrene which, untreated, could have killed him. Padre Pio had wounds in the palms of his hands, in each of his feet, and in his side for fifty years. They never healed and they never became infected!

Padre Pio lost as much as a cup of blood a day. Yet, physicians found his blood work "perfect and "no signs of anemia." The doctors ruled the wounds were not self-inflicted, nor the result of physical or mental disease. They concluded there was no human explanation. Still, the various doctors did not give up and continued to search for answers.

One doctor decided that Padre Pio unconsciously kept them from going away by disinfecting them with iodine. He was sure if the wounds were left alone, they would heal. He ordered that Pio's wounds be bandaged for eight days, with the dressings changed by a group of people so each could watch the others to verify no one let Padre Pio put iodine on his wounds. They testified that the condition of the wounds during the eight days always remained the same. They did not use any medication and, even though they trusted Padre Pio completely, in order to avoid the slightest suspicion, took away the iodine that he kept in his room. After eight days the bandaged wounds were bleeding more than ever.

Pio tried to hide his hands and feet, but it was impossible to hide the bleeding all the time even though he wore half gloves on his hands and dark stockings on his feet. The young seminarians were curious.

"Father, what is going on?" they asked repeatedly but stopped troubling him when they saw how much their questions upset him.

"Boys, please do not discuss this with anyone," he begged.

They wanted to follow his directions, but as their families came to visit, they could not keep this news to themselves. Soon the whole village knew and word was spreading fast to the nearest city, Foggio, and on to Naples.

In Naples the owner of a daily newspaper heard about it and sent one of his top writers to check this out. The journalist spent hours talking to Pio personally. He could see this man was not a charlatan, but a simple, warm-hearted priest who loved God and everyone around him.

Then a miracle happened in front of the journalist's eyes—a crippled man, ordered by Padre Pio, "Come on, walk," overcame his fear of falling, dropped his crutches, and stepped forward! His foot mangled in an accident had been healed! The writer reported what he had learned to his editor and the article was printed in the newspaper. In a short time, Padre Pio's secret became known throughout the world!

Chapter 8

A Poor Friar Who Prays

Padre Pio was no longer just another priest praying in the friary as he wished to be. The news of the stigmata had spread all over. This young man only wanted to do God's will, but what was God's purpose in giving him the stigmata? How did it change him and his world?

Though Padre Pio would live for fifty more years —his life was not easy He continually suffered great pain. His white bandages were always red, covered with blood. His feet hurt so much that he could hardly walk, but his mind was clear and his heart was open. Now, not only the villagers, but also people from all over who heard of the stigmata and his holiness came to him for advice. Sinners, as well as ordinary men and women wanted to confess to him. They took long difficult journeys and endured waits in line for hours, days, and even a month just to confess to him. To some he was stern, to others kind depending on their need.

Sometimes he would hear confessions as many as 15 hours a day and he would only spend a few minutes with each. He would grow very weary.

Imagine being in the dark confessional all day, listening to penitents without a break. After a while, it would seem you would not be able to think! Yet with the Lord's help, he could stand it and he guided many souls—both people of faith and those with none—to God. In the course of his lifetime about five million are known to have entered his confessional!

For many years, at times falsely accused, Pio was being watched and studied by the Franciscans and by the Church. There were constant investigations and inquiries. Several Popes isolated him from the people he loved and there were times he was not allowed to say Mass publicly or hear confessions, and even forbidden to reply to any of the many letters he received.

Because of all the commotion about him he was ordered removed to another friary more than once, but thousands of villagers of San Giovanni Rotondo would climb the mountainside, protest loudly, block the doors, and surround the friary doing anything they could to prevent his leaving. He was their saint!

Eventually, they were successful and the Franciscans decided he was meant to remain at Our Lady of Grace.

Though the villagers could not understand, Pio accepted whatever came as he knew the Church was trying to protect the faithful from what might be trickery or deception. Though the people unofficially canonized him, his superiors had to wait for God's time. They believed if he was truly a saint, time would prove it.

This friar was cheerful and jovial with a wonderful sense of humor. If, by chance, you were in the area, and stumbled upon him in the garden, you might see him praying the Stations or kneeling before a grotto. He would not be sad that you interrupted him. He would probably turn to you with a smile, give you a rose, and pat you on the head. Perhaps he would sit with you on a bench and tell you a funny story. Like

St. Francis of Assisi, he might tell the noisy birds to hush so you could hear him, or take your hand and lead you down the garden path to the chapel. Yes, he carried a cross like Jesus did all the days of his life, but you would never know it.

In the fifty years after the stigmata when he was unable to leave the friary, he continued to appear in various places around Italy, hearing a confession in St. Peter's in Rome or comforting the dying, miles from San Giovanni Rotondo.

Once during World War II, when planes were scheduled to dump bombs near San Giovanni Rotondo, the pilots saw in the sky a friar who told them "GO BACK!" The squad looked at each other in disbelief and dropped the bombs in the ocean. Later, some of them were on leave and decided to visit the friary. There they attended Mass and met Padre Pio afterward. Immediately, they looked at each other.

"By God, do you know who this is? I can't believe it! This is the friar we saw in the sky!" they told each other.

Others soldiers were guided from danger by a strange friar who disappeared after rescuing them. Later, they too would recognize Padre Pio as the one who guided them to safety. There were many other occasions where he would be recognized far away while his body was back in the friary lying on his bed or in the chapel saying Mass.

This blessed man was also able to predict future events, knowing in advance that Hitler would not develop the atomic bomb in time to devastate the world, that Mussolini "wouldn't die in bed," and Cardinal Montini would become Pope Paul VI. Some even say that he predicted Karol Wojtyla, who visited him many times, would become the future Pope John Paul II.

God gave him these gifts called "prophecy," "bi-location," and "reading minds" to carry out His work. Another gift was a strange one—the gift of perfume —a flowery fragrance that was obvious to those around him. At one point his superior cautioned him about this.

"Pio," he was told, "a friar does not wear perfume!"
—But then this friar never did!

Though Pio was known throughout the world, he always stayed close to his family. Many times over the years his mother came to visit at San Giovanni Rotondo. In December 1928, she decided she would spend the holiday season with her Franci. Maria stayed nearby at the comfortable home of a good woman whose two-story house in the village was always open to pilgrims. The pine branches were laden with snow and the month of December was freezing cold on the mountain. Maria, who had not brought warm clothing, caught double pneumonia not long after she arrived. On Christmas Eve, icy winds were blowing.

"Maria, you are very weak. It is best that you stay home tonight, pleaded her friend.

Maria was longing to visit the Manger and hear the choir sing carols as her son said midnight Mass, so she did not listen. The scent of the pine decorations and the beauty of the candlelight warmed her heart. After Mass the howl of wolves sounded throughout the forest. She felt a cold chill as she tightened her scarf and pulled her thin coat close to her. Pio helped her onto the cart taking her to her friend's warm home where she huddled under the covers, and never got up again.

Everyday, her Franci came to be with her. Nine days after that Christmas morning, the wind was still howling and heavy snow was falling as Pio came to her bedside. He bent to kiss her and noticed her skin was cool and her breathing was getting shallow. The end was near! He gave his mother the Last Sacraments and kissed her once more. Then he fainted. When he came to, he lay on the bed beside her and held her cold white hand in his. Candles shone on her face as prayers were said around her bed. Then she lifted the crucifix to her lips, closed her eyes and died. He reached over and held her in his arms. "Mammella, Mammella," he sobbed. "Oh my beautiful Mama!"

Tears streamed down his cheeks. He couldn't stop crying. Another friar, who had come with him that morning, admonished him.

"But, dear father, you yourself teach that suffering must not be anything other then an expression of love which we offer to God, so why are you crying?"

"Oh Brother, don't you understand, my dear mother is gone. It is so hard to bear. Can't you see, Brother, these are tears of love and nothing other than love?" was his anguished reply.

Pio collapsed and was unable to return to the friary or even attend her funeral. For days he wept.

After Mama Forgione died, Grazio left his little home in Pietrelcina and came to live permanently in the home of the same woman who had cared for his wife. Father and son spent many hours together. Finally, his many years of hard work on the farm and in America took a toll on him. Grazio grew old and tired. Each day Pio, himself frail, trudged down the mountain from the friary to help tend him and pray with him. Eighteen years after his mother died, Pio lit the holy candles again and gave his father the Last Sacraments "Oh, my papa, my papa," he wept as his father who had become so close to him slipped away. He was heavy with sorrow. For over a week after the funeral, he could only get up from his bed to say Mass. Padre Pio knew it was God's will, but like all of us when we lose someone we love, his heart was aching for a long time.

Chapter 9

AN IMPOSSIBLE DREAM

Although Padre Pio lived in constant pain from the stigmata and his frequent bouts with the devil who would not let him alone, he did not feel anyone should go looking for suffering or not try to relieve it. One day a woman came to him and said she wanted to suffer for Jesus so she was going to eat some poisonous plants.

"I will not permit this madness," Pio roared at her. "It is up to God to give us a cross. If he hasn't sent you one it is because He is not sure you could bear it."

Padre Pio felt it was the work of the Christian to relieve suffering of others in the world. When people came to him, troubled in mind or body, he prayed for them and put them in touch with others who could help them.

He tried to give them direction to find a medical cure, and in his heart he had a secret dream.

This dream first came to him in the early part of 1920 when a man was seriously hurt in a mine accident near San Giovanni Rotondo. Sirens screamed and lights flashed as an ambulance rushed him over dirt roads to the nearest town forty miles away for medical treatment. A week later, a woman rushed down the stone path to Pio as he was leaving the chapel. She touched his arm as she brushed aside her tears.

"What is it, my child?" he asked as his penetrating eyes searched her face.

"Father, you must pray for my husband," the wife pleaded. "The mine accident, remember? He is in the Foggio hospital, but it is so crowded that he's on a cot in the corridor. The doctors have stopped the bleeding, but they are so busy with all the others, they don't do anything for him. I can see he is failing! Oh, Father, I am so afraid he's never going to come home to me!"

Padre Pio's heart was touched. He knelt on the ground, took out his rosary and prayed with her. He knew the sick and injured of San Giovanni needed more than prayers. Even though he himself had the gift of healing people, he knew this was not the answer. Something must be done for his people. They needed a hospital! He wondered what he, a Capuchin priest bound by a vow of poverty, could do? He prayed continually about this.

God would eventually answer his prayer, but it did not happen overnight. It took a long time for things to work out. In fact, it took many years. After World War II came and devastated Italy, hundreds of the injured passed through San Giovanni. A hospital was badly needed, but still it seemed God was not ready.

At last the time was right. On January 9, 1946 three friends who were doctors gathered together with Pio in his cell at Our Lady of Grace. They listened to his dream and discussed ways to make it a reality.

"I have been thinking about this for a long time. We must do something soon," Padre Pio told them. "We need care for the sick right here. I see this as a special hospital. It won't be cold and clinical. I picture small wards, soft colors, flowers for the patients. Faith and hope will make their spirits well... science, if it can, will do the rest."

As the physicians sat around his bed, studying

plans, and pondering how such an idea was possible, Pio suddenly turned to one of the doctors.

"You will come and live at San Giovanni Rotondo," he told him.

"Oh, Father," he answered, "I can't do that. I am too poor to retire."

Padre Pio told him. "Well, there is the ticket..."

"Ticket, what ticket?" asked the puzzled doctor. There was no reply.

The meeting was over: they all picked up their papers, packed their brief cases, and returned home with that question unanswered. You can imagine this doctor's shock one day not long after when he was back in his office caring for his patients. The mailman brought an official-looking envelope marked "Urgent" to his desk. He finished with his patient and quickly pulled out his letter opener. He read the words over and over.

"My God, Pio knew!" he thought. "I can't believe it! I've won a fortune! Now I will retire and move to San Giovanni!"

He reached for his phone to give Pio the good news and tell him he would he giving most of the money to the new hospital. That was the beginning of the dream's realization. After years of persistence, God granted Pio's wish. The doctors spread the news. Small and large donations came from all over the world. Soon construction began. The hospital was built high on a rocky barren mountain where moving building materials was almost impossible but, as was found out, all things are possible through God. An added blessing was that this work, plus installing water and electricity to serve the hospital, gave work to the poor villagers.

Ten years later (on May 5, 1956) it happened! The House for the Relief of Suffering was officially opened. That day, a happy Padre Pio prayed. "May it be a place of prayer and science... In every sick man there is Jesus... suffering; ... every poor man is Jesus himself... And so was born a hospital on a mountain that no one thought was possible—in fact, many said was "crazy"—one that has the finest doctors, nurses, and equipment ready to serve the sick and needy. Rich and poor, native or foreigner receive the same loving care. No one waits in the corridor of this hospital! Padre Pio's dream-come-true is the present day Good Samaritan.

Chapter 10

IN JESUS YOU WILL FIND ME

As we already know. Padre Pio had the gift of prophecy. Once, in a conversation he had predicted he would die in his 81st year. Another time, he mentioned he'd die when the crypt of the new church was blessed. On Sunday morning, September 22, 1968, the new church at San Giovanni Rotondo was blessed. The baby "with the white veil," Francis Forgione, had lived for 81 years and 4 months. He had "become great." No one could doubt the midwife's prediction. Now that child was old and frail.

Although he still said Mass, he often had to be carried to the altar. After Mass that morning, he fell. He looked up to the crucifix with tear-filled eyes and pleaded, "Dear Lord, I can't take it any more!"

God has promised He will never give us a cross we cannot bear. Pio was ready to go home to God. He spent the day in his cell resting. As evening darkened the sky, he lifted his head from his pillow.

"I want you to hear my confession," he told the friar who sat with him.

After he had confessed, Padre Pio told him, "I want to die in my habit."

The young friar removed the robe from a chair and helped him dress for the last time. As he placed Pio's arms in the sleeves, he remembered a conversation they had had not long before.

The friar had asked, "Father, what will we do without you?"

Pio's answer was, "In Jesus you will find me."

Pio knew his time had come. He got out of bed and struggled to the window of his little room. He looked out onto the terrace at the crowd of pilgrims who still waited there. With a smile, he painfully lifted his hand, blessed them, and fell back on his bed. Padre Pio, who loved the Blessed Mother, held his rosary tightly in his hands and stopped breathing at 2:30 AM. "Gesu... Maria," were his last words.

Shortly before his death, the father guardian of the friary and the doctor had been called to the cell. They noticed that the wounds had begun to close, and the bleeding was almost gone. When Pio died, they saw the skin was completely healed. There were no scabs, no scars—no sign they had ever been there. There was a radiance about his body and almost before their eyes, the stigmata had totally disappeared!

Four days later, a hundred thousand persons came to his funeral. In the blue sky overhead, airplanes flew in formation and bowed their wings.

"Children," Padre Pio once said. "You have come into the world as I have, with a mission to accomplish." You have heard this mysterious story of the stigmata. You will have to draw your own conclusions as to why this young man was given so much suffering. Padre Pio was only different from you and me in that he prayed constantly—all day, every day—in words and actions. He was one with Jesus and came as a messenger to teach us to be holy and have a holy influence. Perhaps in learning how he bore his pain and suffering, we can rise above our own pain and go on as he did—to still accomplish great things in our time on earth. Perhaps that is how Padre Pio could suffer so much physical agony and embarrassment and still love God. It was his mission in life! Now you must discover yours.

Postscript

Many miracles were attributed to Padre Pio both before and after his death on September 23, 1968. On May 2, 1999 Pope John Paul II declared him "Blessed." On June 16, 2002 hundreds of thousands exulted in St. Peter's Square in Rome and throughout the world as Pope John Paul II formally declared him a saint.

Chronology

1887	May 25	Francis is born in Pietrelcina to Grazio and Maria Forgione.
	May 26	Baptized in the Church of St. Mary of the Angels.
1897	May	Received First Holy Communion.
1899	Sept. 27	Received Sacrament of Confirmation
1903	Jan. 6	Enters the Capuchin friary at Morcone.
	Jan. 22	Recives habit and religious name, Fra Pio.
1910	Sept. 20	Receives temporary invisible stigmata.
1915	Nov. 15	Drafted into the Italian Army.
1918	Mar. 16	Honorably discharged from the army. REturns to San Giovanni Rotondo.
	Sept. 20	Receives the visible marks of the stimgata.
1919	May 15	Fr. Provincial has Luigi Romanelli investigate the stigmata.
	July 26	Professor Amico Bignami examines him.
	Oct. 9	Dr. George Festa examines him.
1920	April 18	Fr. Augostino Gemelli, OFM attempts examination; claims they are a fraud. His report impresses Pope Pius XI.
	July 15	Examination by Dr. Festa and Prof. Romanelli.

The Way of the Cross

1923	May 31	First decree ordering isolation of Padre Pio. He may celebrate Mass only in the friary private chapel with no one attending. May not respond to anyletters.
1924	July 24	Second decree against Padre Pio.
1926	Apr. 23	Third decree against Padre Pio.
	July 11	Fourth decree against Padre Pio.
1929	Jan. 3	Death of Padre Pio's mother.
1933	July 16	Pope Pius XI reinstates Padre Pio.
1940	Jan. 9	First meeting of the committee for construction of The House for the Suffering. Formation of Prayer Groups.
1946	Oct. 7	Death of his father Grazio.
1947	May 19	Ground breaking for construction of The Hospital for the Relief of Suffering.
1956	May 5	The House for the Relief of Suffering is opened.
1968	Sept. 23	Padre Pio dies.
	Sept. 26	Padre Pio's funeral. He is laid to rest in the crypt of the church.
1999	May 2	Beatification of Padre Pio at St. Peter's in Rome by Pope John Paul II.
2002	June 16	Canonization of Padre Pior in Rome by Pope John Paul II.

A Miracle

Can a person without pupils see? The answer given by any ophthalmologist is, "It is not possible." Once there was a little girl named Gemma di Giorgi who was born blind. Her eyes had no pupils. In 1947 when she was seven years old, her grandmother decided to take her to San Giovanni Rotondo to see Padre Pio. She was praying for a miracle. They lived in Sicily and had to go by ship to Foggia. As they were cruising along, Gemma told her grandmother she could see the sea and a steamboat. Other pilgrims who were with them began to speak of a miracle. The grandmother, who was tired and exhausted by the trip, seemed unable to comprehend it.

When she arrived at the monastery, she went to confession with Padre Pio and asked him to give eyesight to her grandchild. She told him that Gemma was weeping because she had forgotten to ask for this when she went to confession. Pio answered her, "Do you have faith, my daughter? The child must not weep and neither must you for the child sees, and you know she sees!" Later Padre Pio gave Gemma her First Holy Communion and made a cross over her eyes and they set out for home.

During the trip the grandmother became ill with a high fever and had to go to the hospital. As soon as she recovered, she had Gemma's eyes examined by an eye specialist who immediately declared Gemma blind and without pupils. The grandmother became confused when the oculist declared Gemma blind. She insisted to the doctor that the child could see. The doctor then showed Gemma some objects and when she recognized them and showed distinctly and without difficulty that she saw these things, the doctor said, "Without pupils, one cannot see. This child sees. It is a miracle!" Since that time many eye doctors from all over Italy have examined Gemma's eyes. Many have even come to their home and all have declared the same thing, "Without pupils in one's eyes, one should not be able to see."

Gemma who lives in Ribera, Sicily, is now 82 years old. The girl who was born without pupils still sees!

Padre Pio's Prayer

This is the prayer which Padre Pio recited everyday for all those who asked his prayers.

O my Jesus, you have said. "Truly I say to you, ask and it will be given you, seek and you will find, knock and it will be opened to you." Behold I knock, I seek and ask for the grace of... *Our Father... Hail Mary... Glory be to the Father... Sacred Heart of Jesus, I place my trust in you.*

O my Jesus, you have said, "Truly I say to you, if you ask anything of the Father in my name, he will give it to you." Behold, in your name, I ask the Father the grace of... *Our Father... Hail Mary... Glory be to the Father... Sacred Heart of Jesus, I place my trust in you.*

O my Jesus, you have said, "Truly I say to you, heaven and earth will pass away but my words will not pass away." Encouraged by your infallible words, I now ask for the grace of... *Our Father... Hail Mary... Glory be to the Father... Sacred Heart of Jesus, I place my trust in you.*

O Sacred Heart of Jesus, for whom it is impossible not to have compassion on the afflicted, have pity on us miserable sinners and grant us the grace which we ask of you through the Sorrowful and Immaculate Heart of Mary, your tender Mother and ours. *Hail. Holy Queen... St. Joseph, foster-father of Jesus, pray for us.*

www.ingramcontent.com/pod-product-compliance
Lightning Source LLC
Chambersburg PA
CBHW070653050426
42451CB00008B/337